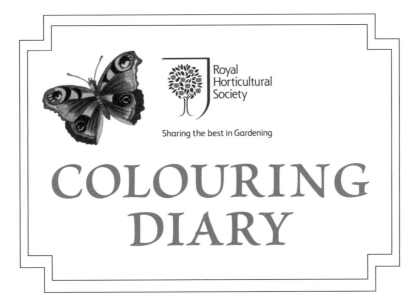

Royal
Horticultural
Society

Sharing the best in Gardening

COLOURING
DIARY

Michael O'Mara Books Limited

First published in Great Britain in 2016 by
Michael O'Mara Books Limited
9 Lion Yard
Tremadoc Road
London SW4 7NQ

A CIP catalogue record for this book is available from the British Library.

ISBN: 978-1-78243-641-6

1 2 3 4 5 6 7 8 9 10

www.mombooks.com

All colour images copyright of the RHS Lindley Library
available at www.rhsimages.co.uk

Black-and-white illustrations by Gavin Rutherford, Julie Ingham,
Oana Befort, Pimlada Phuapradit, Zoe Connery

Cover illustration by Pimlada Phuapradit

Designed by Ana Bjezancevic

Printed in Spain by Graficas Estella

January

1	**2**
3	**4**
5	**6**
7	

January

8

9

10

11

12

13

14

January

15

16

17

18

19

20

21

notes

January

22

23

24

25

26

27

28

January

29	30

31

February

1

2

3

4

5

6

7

February

8

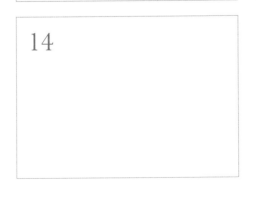

9

10

11

12

13

14

February

15

16

17

18

19

20

21

notes

February

22	23
24	25
26	27
28	29

March

1

2

3

4

5

6

7

March

8	
9	
10	
11	

12

13

14

notes

March

15	16
17	18
19	20
21	

March

22

23

24

25

26

27

28

March

29	30 
31	

April

1

2

3

4

5

6

7

notes

April

8

9

10

11

12

13

14

April

15

16

17

18

19

20

21

April

22

23

24

25

26

27

28

29

30

notes

May

1

2

3

4

5

6

7

May

8

9

10

11

12

13

14

May

15

16

17

18

19

20

21

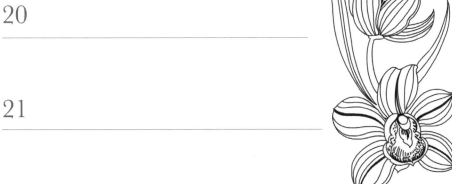

May

22

23

24

25

26

27

28

notes

May

29

30

31

June

1

2

3

4

5

6

7

June

8

9

10

11

12

13

14

June

15

16

17

18

19

20

21

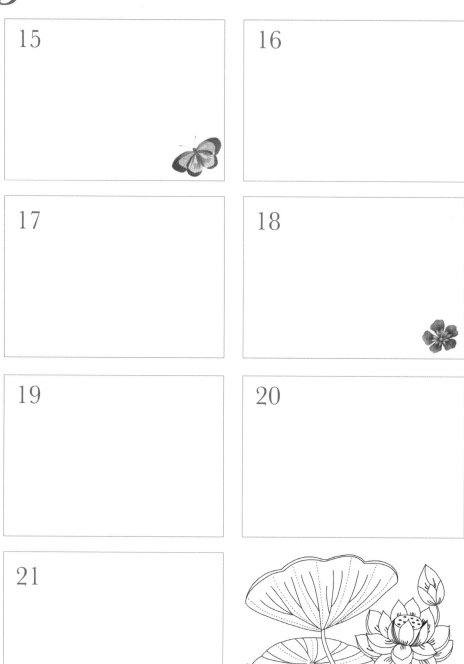

June

22

23

24

25

26

27

28

29

30

notes

July

1

2

3

4

5

6

7

July

8 _____

9 _____

10 _____

11 _____

12 _____

13 _____

14 _____

July

15	
16	
17	
18	

19

20

21

notes

July

22	23
24	25
26	27
28	

July

29

30

31

notes

August

1

2

3

4

5

6

7

notes

August

8

9

10

11

12

13

14

August

15

16

17

18

19

20

21

August

22	23

24	25

26	27

28

August

29	30

31

September

1

2

3

4

5

6

7

September

8	9
10 	11
12	13
14	

September

15
_____

16
_____

17
_____

18
_____

19
_____

20
_____

21
_____

September

22

23

24

25

26

27

28

29

30

notes

October

1

2

3

4

5

6

7

notes

October

8

9

10

11

12

13

14

October

15 _____

16 _____

17 _____

18 _____

19 _____

20 _____

21 _____

October

22

23

24

25

26

27

28

29

30

31

notes

November

1

2

3

4

5

6

7

November

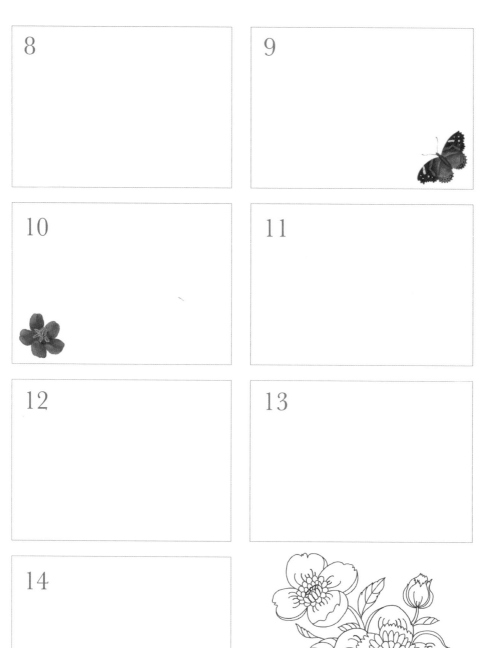

8

9

10

11

12

13

14

November

15 _____

16 _____

17 _____

18 _____

19 _____

20 _____

21 _____

November

22

23

24

25

26

27

28

notes

November

29	30

notes

December

1	2
3	4
5	6
7	

December

8

9

10

11

12

13

14

# December

15

16

17

18

19

20

21

December

22

23

24

25

26

27

28

29

30

31

notes

Year Planner

January

February

March

April

May

June

July

August

September

October

November

December

Notes

Notes

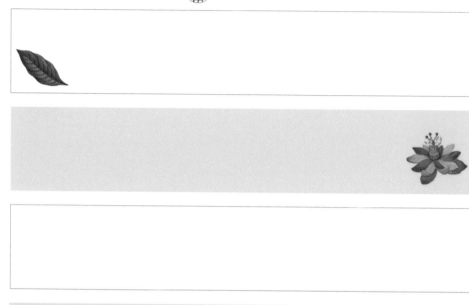